Can People Ever Go Back in Time?

Children's Physics of Energy

Speedy Publishing LLC
40 E. Main St. #1156
Newark, DE 19711
www.speedypublishing.com

People sometimes wish there was a way to go back in time to see and feel how things were in the ancient times or maybe for the purpose of keeping disasters or mistakes from happening.

Even though there are many fictional stories of time travel adventures, no one has yet invented a time machine like the ones we see in the movies.

According to the theories of physics, there are three ways that we could possibly travel back in time.

Go faster than the speed of light.

Time slows down when you travel at speeds approaching the speed of light, relative to the observer.

OCCASVS
CREPVSCVLVM
10
11
12

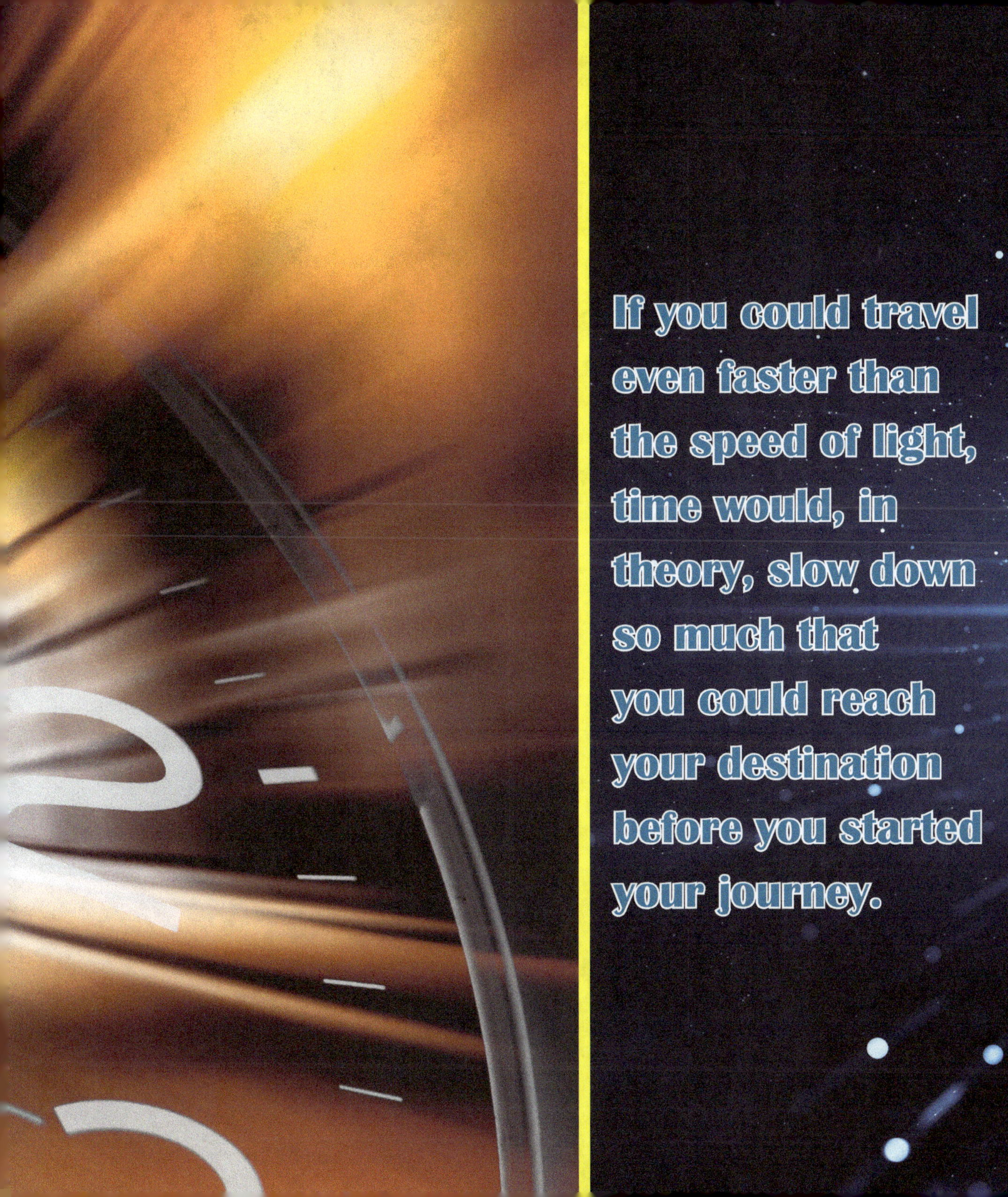

If you could travel even faster than the speed of light, time would, in theory, slow down so much that you could reach your destination before you started your journey.

But this is difficult to achieve because, according to Einstein's Special Theory of Relativity, the faster you go, the more massive you become and more energy is needed to accelerate you further.

Dive into a wormhole.

A wormhole is a theoretical passageway through space and time which could provide shortcuts for journeys across space in the universe. It is believed that wormholes connect distant galaxies in different times.

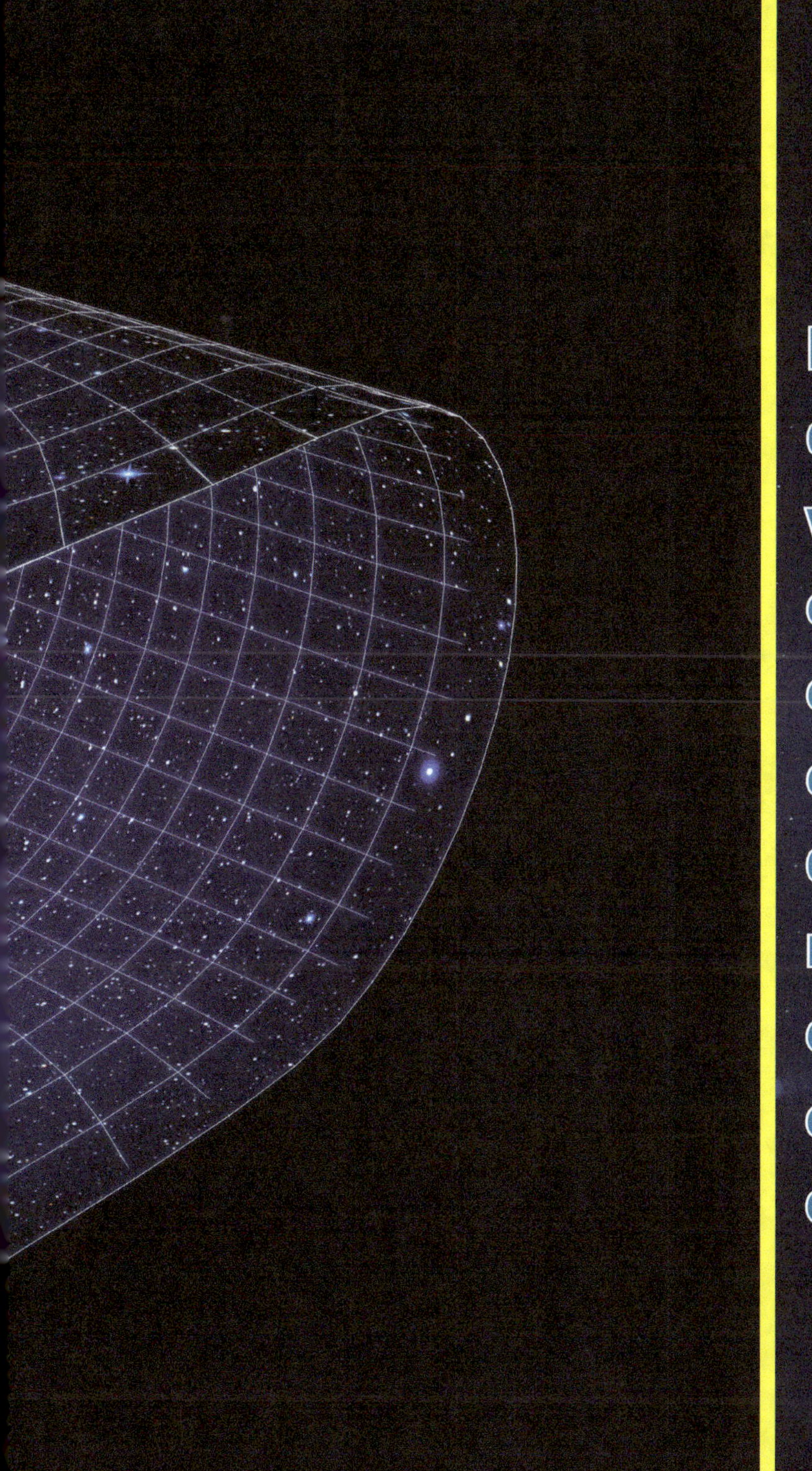

However, there are dangers associated with this. There could be sudden collapses, contact with dangerous exotic materials, and exposure to high concentrations of radiation.

Travel to the future.

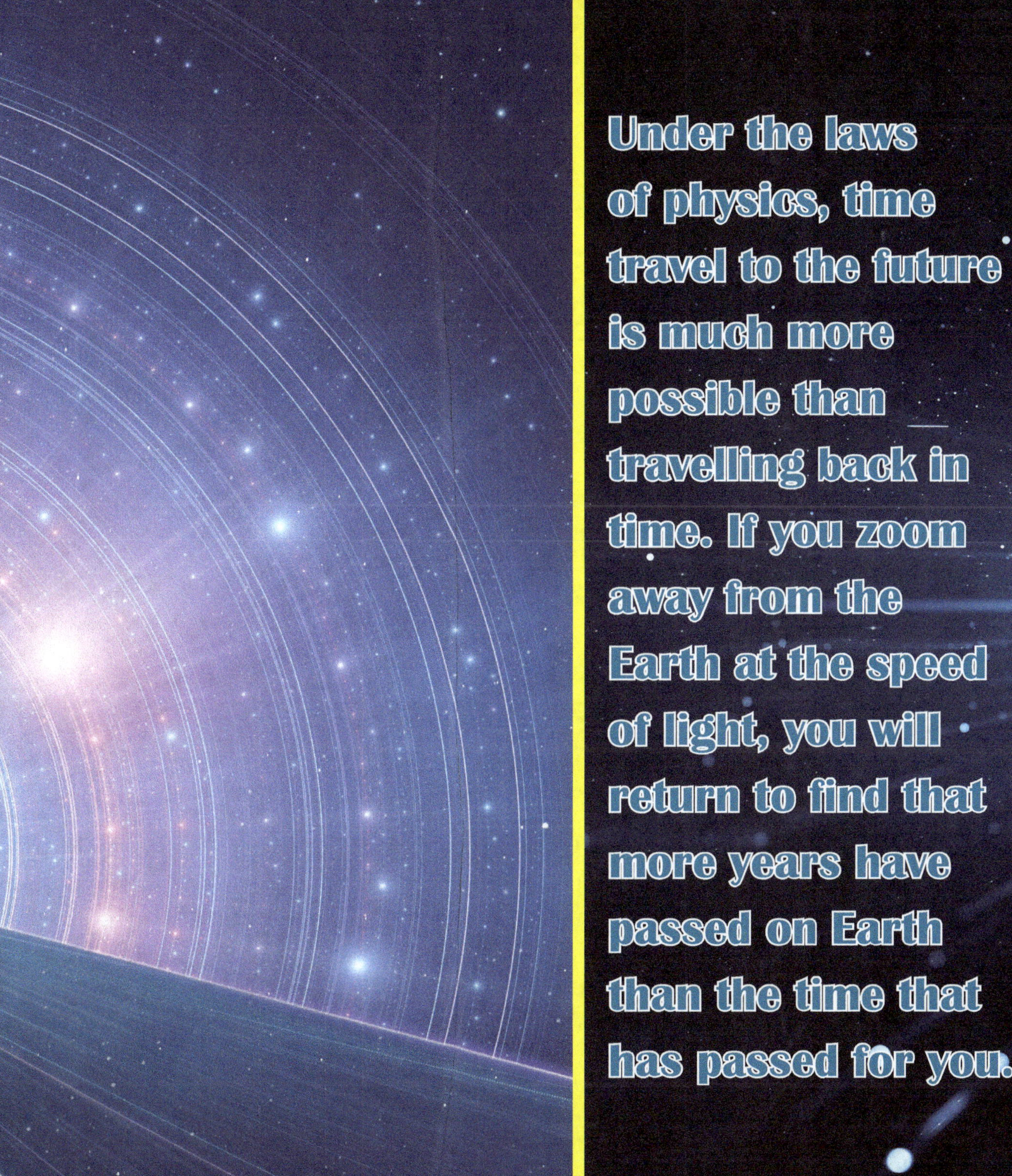

Under the laws of physics, time travel to the future is much more possible than travelling back in time. If you zoom away from the Earth at the speed of light, you will return to find that more years have passed on Earth than the time that has passed for you.

If that's so, then you can go to the future and then perhaps if the people in the future were able to find ways to travel back in time, they could then send you to the time in the past that you would want to go to.

You could also be like Captain America, who was preserved through time with the use of a freezer. However, this technology has hardly been perfected.

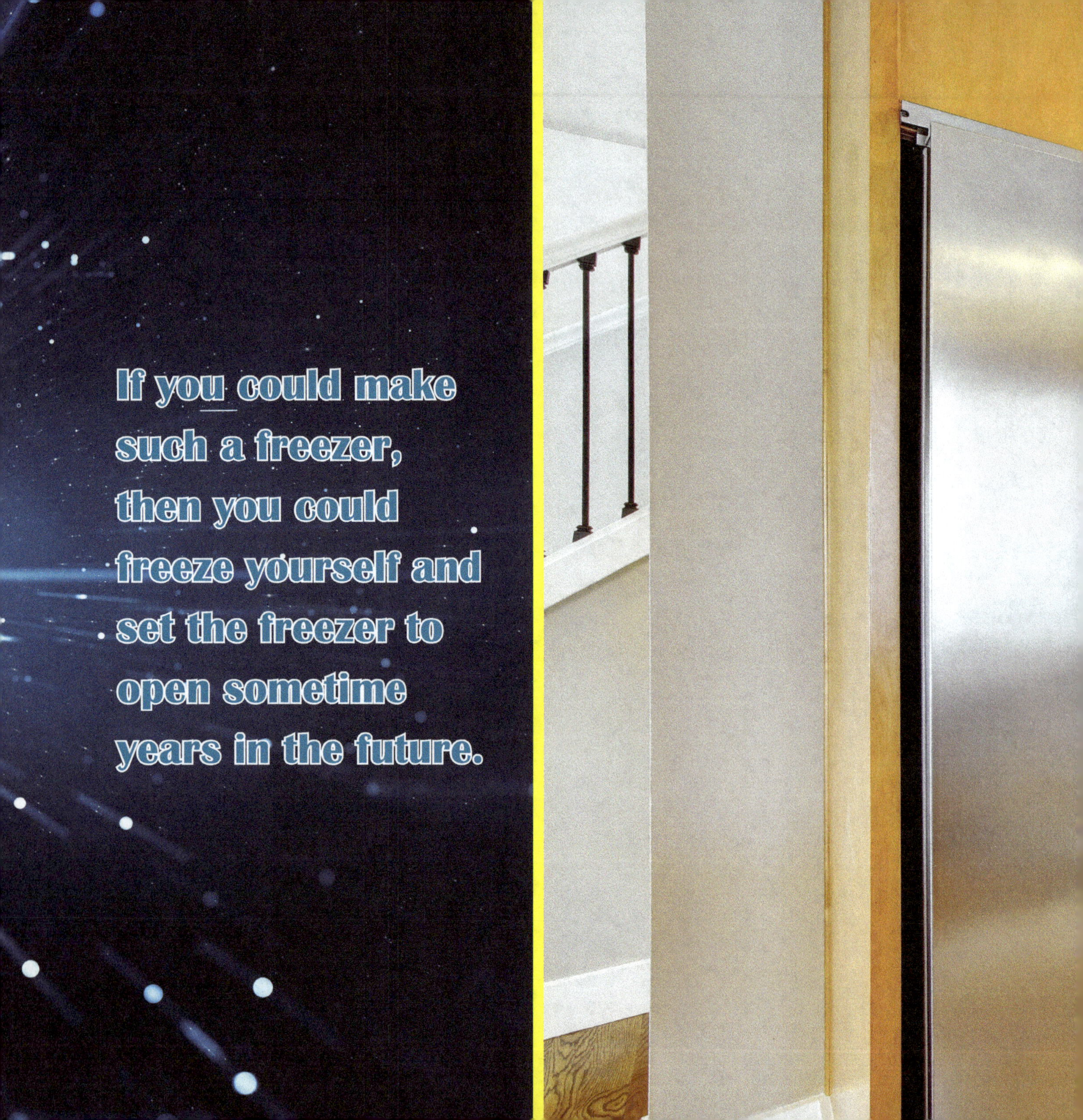

If you could make such a freezer, then you could freeze yourself and set the freezer to open sometime years in the future.

SOMEWHERE 06.06.1966

What is true for now is that we don't have the technology to allow us to travel back in time.

The only thing that we have right now is our imaginations. If you want to remember things that had happened in the past, you can reminisce.

career
SPORT
information

Long-term memories can be hard to dig up but, with some stimuli, you will soon start remembering vivid details and recalling long-forgotten emotions.

These stimuli can be (1) revisiting places where past events took place, (2) calling old contacts, (3) looking at old pictures and mementos, (5) using the same perfume you used to put on, (6) listening to songs you used to love, (7) playing your childhood games, and (8) writing down what you do remember—as you write, you may find you remember more and more.

www.ingramcontent.com/pod-product-compliance
Lightning Source LLC
LaVergne TN
LVHW060831170826
845678LV00010B/1949

9798869444745